Memphis, Tennessee 38117

Copy # 1

HADASSAH:

Esther the Orphan Queen

HADASSAH:

Esther the Orphan Queen

William H. Armstrong

William H. Armstrong

Illustrated by Barbara Ninde Byfield

Doubleday & Company, Inc., Garden City, New York

ISBN: 0-385-08832-9 Trade
0-385-08843-4 Prebound
Library of Congress Catalog Card Number 72-76114
Copyright © 1972 by William H. Armstrong
All Rights Reserved
Printed in the United States of America
9 8 7 6 5 4 3 2

HADASSAH:

Esther the Orphan Queen

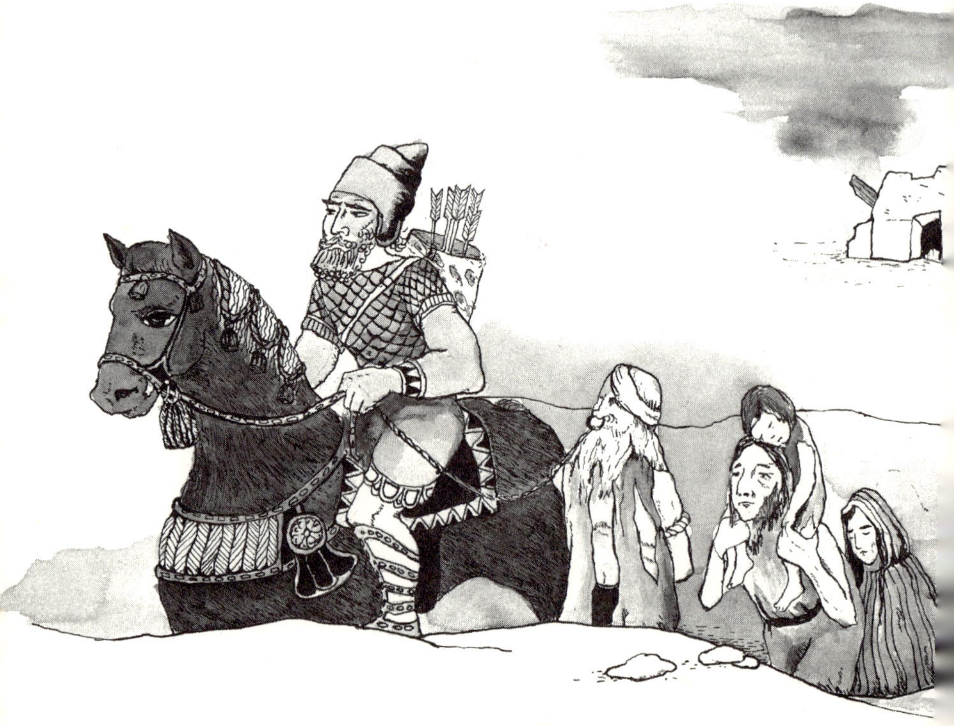

Introduction

I<small>N</small> the whole history of the world there is no story of determination and courage to survive which equals that of the Jewish people. For four thousand years, since Abraham first drove his flocks into that little strip of green land which is called (Israeli) Palestine, their existence has been threatened. Besides the struggle to save their land from the desert people who forever have looked with envy upon the pastures and water holes for their own wandering flocks, the Jewish people have endured slavery in alien lands, oppression under every great empire that has arisen in the Mediterranean and Near Eastern worlds, and time and time again being dispersed over the earth like chaff beaten and scattered by the flail of a merciless thresher.

But they have survived, and that survival is one of history's miracles. If there is an explanation of miracles, this one is explained by a simple faith; that in spite of everything, belief in a just God, and obedience to His commandments, would pull them through. This was the foundation upon which they built their deathless courage. And nowhere in their history is there a more beautiful story of that courage than the story of Esther, the orphan Queen, who saved her people from extermination during a dark period of their history known as the Babylonian Captivity and Exile.

1

Eliezer, the banker, paused briefly at the doorway of the shop that bore the sign of a goldsmith, a scale in which was balanced a small figure of a bull against an equally small cube which represented the value of the bull. "Greetings to my friend, the King's treasure keeper," he said to the man who was approaching from an inner door of the shop with a small olive-wood cylinder in his hand.

"Not the King's treasure keeper," the man replied as he came to the front and stood looking into the street. "A humble appraiser, holding in my hands for the briefest moment and molding for another's pleasure what my friends, the bankers, count and call their own."

"But I would say, Mordecai," replied Eliezer, the banker, lowering his voice and looking both ways in the street, "that there are many times when Eliezer the Jew, would rather be a keeper of sheep or a beekeeper back on the stony hills of the homeland than a banker in this so-called magnificent city of Susa."

A little girl, her tanned cheeks contrasted against the pure white of her tunic, half-glided, half-skipped past the elders as she came from the quarters behind the shop. "Shalom," she greeted them, and then repeated her greeting, "peace be with you" in Persian, *Haoma*. She flicked her head and her long black hair fell into its place about her shoulders.

"Stay near. We must have our lesson before the street is noisy and the sun is high," the man holding the cylindrical olive-wood box with its scroll said as she passed and turned toward the corner of the Street of Awnings. She stepped into the Street of the Sacred Band and began a solitary gazelle-like game of hopscotch, covering the mosaic of a Persian soldier astride a prancing horse in two graceful leaps.

"You're teaching her the language of the Persians?" Eliezer inquired in a tone which was less than sympathetic.

"Yes, and their history," Mordecai replied, and continued, "We are now generations removed from the homeland. The land which our God gave to Moses we have never seen. Our dead are buried here in the land that was Nebuchadnezzar's and is now the Persians'. Cyrus, the Persian, and his successors have shown us kindness. We have been allowed to prosper after the advice and faith of our great prophet Jeremiah to 'Build houses and live in them—seek the welfare of the city where the Lord sent you into exile, and pray to the Lord in its behalf, for in its welfare you will find your welfare—the Lord knows the plans he has for you, plans for welfare and not for evil.' We live as strangers, Eliezer, but not alone. The same God who was with Moses in Egypt is with us here."

"But the customs," Eliezer interrupted, "having to worship our God in secret. And soon the child, now gay and free, will come to the age when that freedom is no more. Persian women are slaves, doomed to view the world darkly through a veil. Your child's bright countenance will be hidden by a Persian veil and her walk will be restricted to the city well and the fish cart."

"But if I teach her the history of this people, she will better understand the customs. And who knows, Eliezer, one day the Persians might understand our customs and our God."

"Your faith is great, Mordecai. Even without your words you show it, standing in the street with the sacred scroll of the Mezuzah in your hand. And its time for the gaushaka, the King's eyes and ears, forever spying, to be in the streets."

"We have our lesson here under the awning, before the sun warms too much, before the streets are thronged."

"But why the useless risk? Behind an inner door I teach my children the one Book and the ways of one people."

"I will not hide my God, Eliezer. The Mezuzah says to me, and the child repeats after me, and openly, in Susa's streets: 'Every place on which the sole of your foot treads shall be yours; your territory shall be from the wilderness and Lebanon and from the river, the river Euphrates to the western sea. No man shall be able to stand against you.' Does that not mean that the Lord shall keep me before my door as easily as behind it? And the child, Esther, now nearing twelve, the age when boys are taken to learn in the temple, I have taught the meaning of the Mezuzah in David's words: 'The Lord shall preserve thy going out and thy coming in from this time forth, even for evermore.'"

"You are a strong fool, Mordecai, my friend. I've tarried too long. I must be at the Counting House."

"You are my friend, Eliezer. My friend whose faith is weak."

Mordecai watched until his friend was gone from view. The street was still quiet. However many things he and Eliezer could not agree on, one thing they did. They met the day early so that neither ever had to hurry to catch the rising sun. Mordecai wondered at Eliezer's discontentment, his calling Susa the "so-called magnificent city."

The Persians were mountain people. When they took Nebuchadnezzar's kingdom, they soon abandoned the cities of the plain and built their cities in the foothills of the Zagros mountains.

Nebuchadnezzar's city of Babylon, which he had proclaimed the world's most beautiful city, was deteriorating. Mordecai had heard it from peddlers and caravan drivers. The terraces upon which Nebuchadnezzar had built his famous Hanging Gardens and planted giant trees "in the sky" were eroding away, the trees sliding into the street as to the bottom of a gorge from some steep precipice. The sixty miles of walls, wide enough for two four-horse chariots to pass on top of them, were sprouting sand briers and thorn bushes in crevices where wind deposited sand and dust from barren fields. For the massive irrigation system that had watered the barley fields and the date and palm trees had filled with silt and dried up. The course of the Euphrates itself had changed, leaving its channel through the heart of the city a collection of stagnant pools surrounded by polluted, malaria-breeding, rank-smelling muck.

Had the prophet not said of the power of Babylon and the splendor of the city: "It shall lie in dust, a place of desolation, and the owl and the jackal shall dwell there."

Mordecai cast his eyes about him at the splendor of Susa. It was only the winter capital, built in the southern region, in the province of Susiana. But it far outstripped Persepolis, the principal capital, in the northern hill country. Everything, structure and activity, bespoke the grandeur and power of the King. Through the city gate galloped the Anagrum, messengers of the King, of whom it was said: "Neither snow, nor rain, nor heat, nor gloom of night" could delay "from the swift completion of their appointed rounds." From the King's one hundred and twenty-seven provinces, stretching from Ethiopia to the Indus River, these couriers brought messages, royal reports, and tribute to the King.

With stone from Armenia, cedarwood from Lebanon, silver and ivory from Africa, and gold from Lydia and Bactria, the city of Susa replaced Babylon as the show place of the Near East. A street paved with glazed brick and inlaid with tile, called the Street of All Countries, led up to the splendid Gate of Xerxes, guarded by massive winged bulls. On a terraced mound behind the gate stood the King's palace with its great hall and throne room, three hundred forty feet long and two hundred forty feet wide. More than a hundred columns, elaborately carved with capitals of palm and lotus leaves and half bulls, lined the hall and supported the roof.

Across a lake formed by bringing the Eulaeus River under the walls of the city, the Queen's palace stood

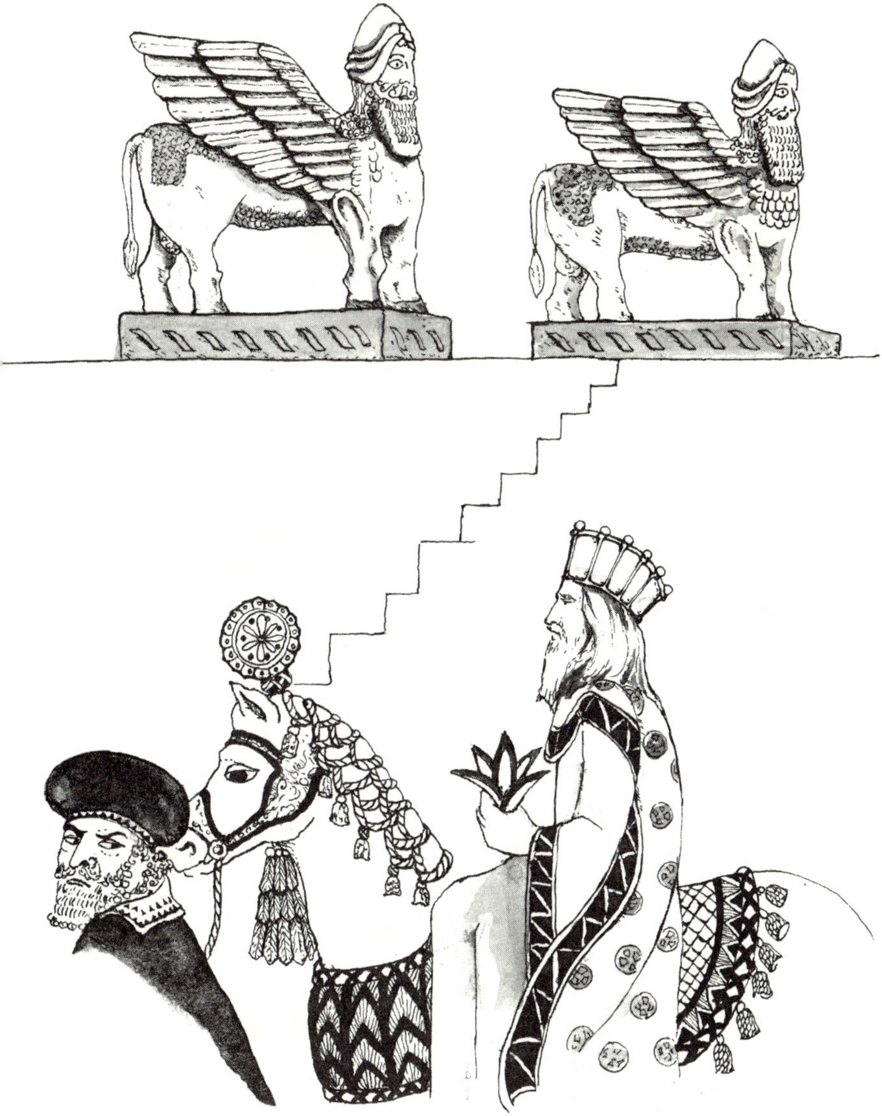

opposite that of the King. The Queen's palace was reached from the outside by the Street of the Sacred Band, named for the elite ten thousand warriors whose lives were sworn to protect the King's life in battle. The Gate of the Golden Spearmen, decorated with reliefs of warriors bearing gold-pointed spears, opened on the terra-cotta and tiled carriage and litter passageways which led through well-groomed gardens to the Queen's palace.

At right angles to the Street of the Sacred Band, just outside the gate, ran the Street of Awnings. Here the tradesmen and craftsmen displayed their wares and carried on business under the many-colored awnings which protected them from Susa's scorching midday sun.

Merchants and adventurers from the many provinces gave the bazaars a carnival-like atmosphere. The varicolored awnings were not to be compared for gaiety to the varied color and style of the clothes worn in the street; from the Persians in their wide-sleeved tunics and balloon-legged trousers to Ethiopians in skins of leopards and lions. Here, too, was to be found the Arab in his zeira, or long cloak; Thracians in suits and boots made of the skin of fawns; Indians in long white tunics; and Jews in simple tunics of natural-colored wool or linen tied at the middle by a girdle of papyrus rope or leather. Here on the Street of Awnings the story of Esther, the orphan Queen, who saved her people, begins.

Mordecai adjusted the prop stakes of the awning. The sun was moving above the roof tops. Peddlers

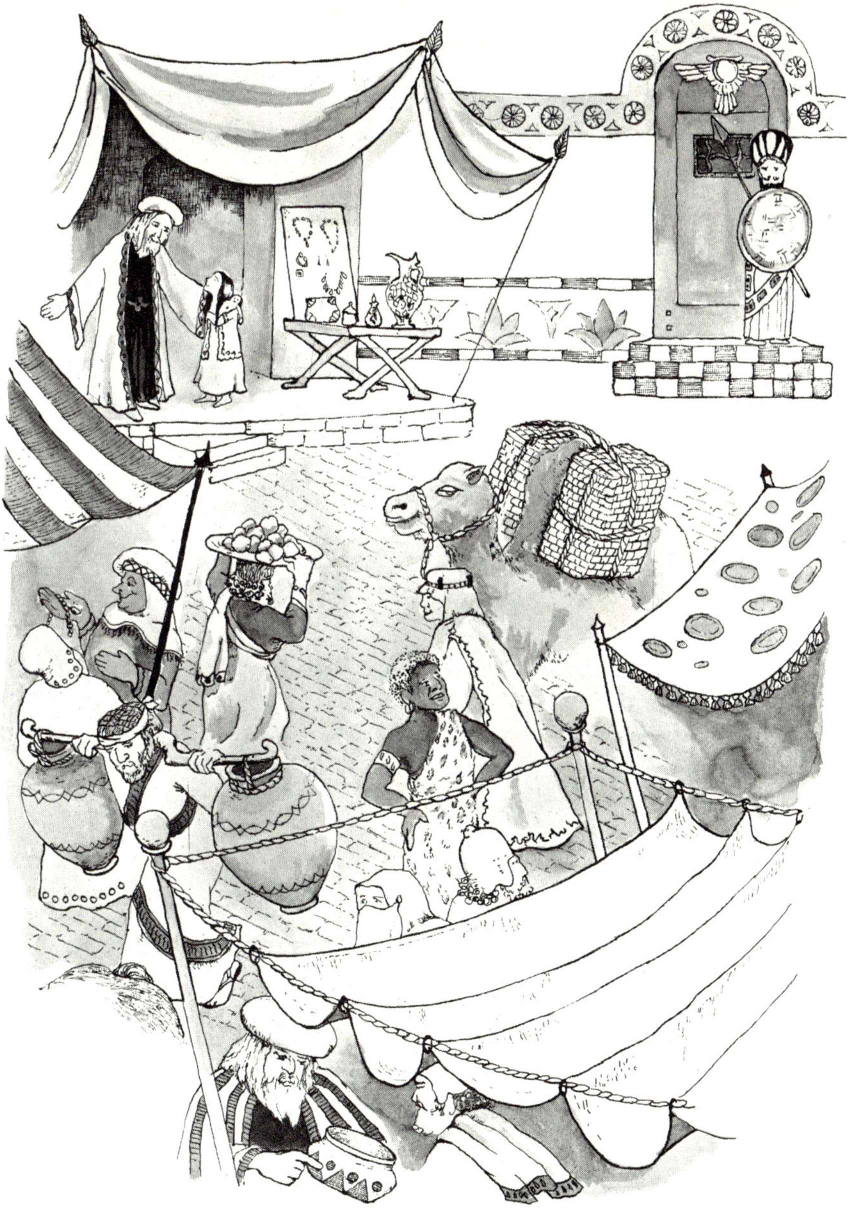

from the country, their backs or burros laden with produce for market, were sifting into the street.

"Come, child," he called to Esther.

When they were seated under the awning, he unrolled the sacred scroll of the Mezuzah and she repeated after him the lesson of the Law and the Book. When they had finished that, he turned to the history lesson for the day. "Cities grow old or they are rooted up and die like men," he began. "But if the Lord builds the city, its workers labor not in vain for it shall yet live. And what city shall live again, as we are told by the prophets?"

"Jerusalem," the child answered.

Teacher and child's attention was drawn to a commotion at the palace gate. Small groups of soldiers were pouring through the gate and turning into the separate streets. At the corner of the Street of Awnings four soldiers stopped to whisper with a Persian in street dress, his wide-sleeved tunic, earthen colored, and his black balloon-legged trousers.

"The gaushaka," the child whispered as the Persian turned into the street and approached. She started to rise. Mordecai pressed her gently back, continuing the lesson. He left the sacred scroll resting where it was unrolled in his lap.

2

THE nearest shop to the Gate of the Golden Spearmen, set under the very shadow of the city wall, belonged to Mordecai. Mordecai had been born in Nippur soon after his father, Jair, a member of the tribe of Benjamin, had been brought with the exiles from Jerusalem and settled there by Nebuchadnezzar. He had been brought up to obey the commandments and worship the one true God. As a youth he had become an apprentice in the bank of Murashu and Sons. There he became an expert appraiser of precious metals and jewels. So when the wise King Darius asked Murashu to recommend someone to become the King's appraiser, Mordecai was given the job.

In order that he might be in a position to see and acquire jewels for the King and Queen brought to the bazaars by traders from the vast reaches of the empire, he was given a shop at the very entrance to the Street of Awnings, right against the Needle's Eye (the small service gate that went through the wall next to the Queen's palace). Here he served Darius, and had continued in the service of Xerxes the seven years since Xerxes had succeeded his father, Darius.

Mordecai also carried on a private business. The traders who came to the bazaar knew only that he was a goldsmith and a buyer and seller of jewels. This had been Xerxes' idea as a way to buy jewels more cheaply, and also to uncover frauds. For crafty merchants sometimes sold golden cups for full weigh of gold when they were really made of lead and plated with gold. These wicked traders, however, were never able to fool Mordecai. If weight and size seemed slightly out of order to Mordecai, he would tap the surface, then hold his ear against it to detect the deadened sound of dross metal concealed in the base or handle. When emeralds and rubies of great size, or transparent jade from the Far East, were brought by the caravans, Mordecai would send quickly for Hegai, the chief custodian of the Queen's palace. Mordecai's keen eye and wise judgments brought great praise from Hegai, and often a word of thanks from Queen Vashti herself was sent by Hegai when he came to the shop of his friend.

Sometime before Mordecai had moved from Nippur to Susa he had become the guardian of his cousin Abihail's daughter, the child Esther. Her mother and father had died in one of the plagues, probably malaria, which brought death to the river valley cities, especially in years when the snows in the mountains of Armenia were not heavy. Then in late summer the Euphrates and Tigris rivers, because there was not enough melting snow to feed them, shrank within their banks to a series of stagnant pools, oozing indifferently toward the Persian Gulf.

Mordecai had adopted Esther as his daughter, and loved her as his very own, for he was old and childless. He taught her the commandments and the customs of her people. He instilled in her the feeling that in a very special way she belonged to a proud people whom God had chosen for His own; and that if they loved Him He would always be with them, wherever they were, and save them however much they were troubled and oppressed.

As a little girl Esther had played under the awning of the shop. She had held precious gems in her tiny fingers, with Mordecai often wishing that they could be hers.

Now grown into a beautiful and graceful maiden, she walked veiled, which was the custom of the women of the city. It was considered very wrong for a woman to be seen with her face uncovered in public. As a child Esther had also hopped and skipped over the glazed inlaid figures on the Street of the Sacred Band. But now, being grown up, she never ventured past the corner of the Street of Awnings. No women except the Queen and members of the King's harem were allowed on the Street of the Sacred Band.

Xerxes, the King, had acquired the reputation of often being too quick to act and too cruel in his actions. This was shown by his action at one of his great festivals. Princes, army chiefs, nobles, and governors from the hundred and twenty-seven provinces of the empire were gathered to the palace to feast their eyes upon the splendor and pomp of his majesty, and their appetites upon the King's food from silver plates and his wine from golden cups. The imperial banqueting lasted a hundred and eighty days.

When the royal feasting ended, Xerxes then ordered a seven-day feast for all the men of Susa "both great and small." The gates to the court of the palace stood open; and in the garden, decorated with hangings of blue and white, tied with cords of purple drawn through silver rings, the people leaned against marble pillars or reclined on couches inlaid with gold and silver, drinking royal wine from goblets of gold. At the same time Queen Vashti gave a small banquet for the women assigned to her palace.

On the last day of the feast "when the King's heart was merry with wine" he became boisterous and loud, announcing that all should see the most beautiful woman in the Kingdom, Queen Vashti. This was a clear indication that he had drunk too much, for women never lifted their veils in the presence of men other than their husbands.

Xerxes sent his chief messenger to tell the Queen to come to the feast. He also sent six attendants with the royal litter to carry her.

Vashti was indeed a beautiful woman. She was also a wise lady. She heard the request with disgust and indignation, knowing full well that the King would never have made it if he had not had too much to drink. To appear unveiled before the men of Susa and the King's officers would disgrace her forever in

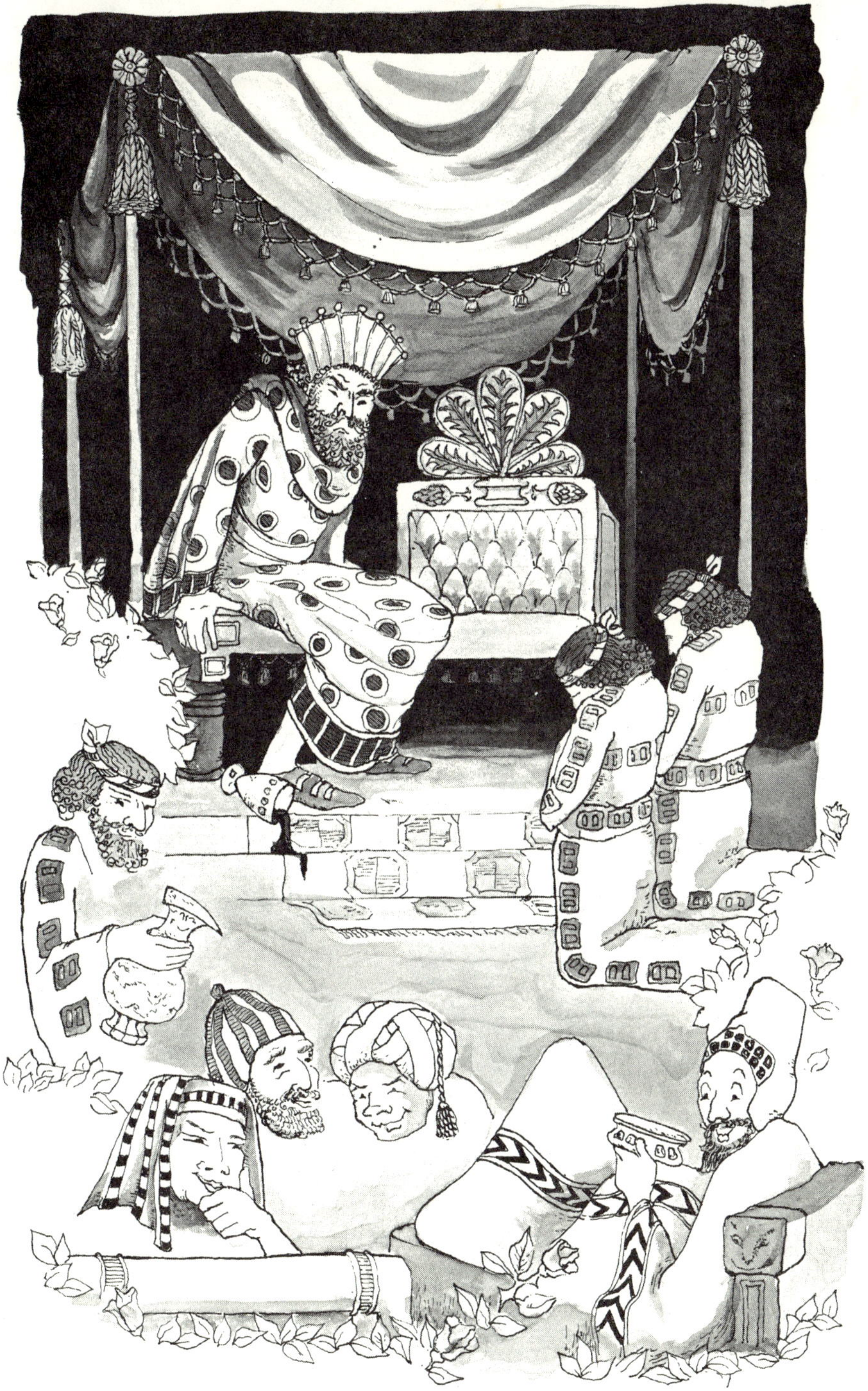

the eyes of her subjects, especially the women who honored and revered her. She sent back word that she would not violate one of the women's most sacred customs.

Now the Persian King's order was equal to a law, for whatever the King spoke became law the minute it was uttered. It could not be retracted. The King was so powerful that a simple wave of his scepter or nod of his head could decree the execution of one person, or many, without a trial.

When he heard that Vashti would not come, he was enraged and angered. He repeated over and over in a loud voice, "The King's word is above custom; the King's word is law. The King who changes the geography of the land from its farthest reaches can change customs."

If only the messenger and litter bearers had heard the King, he could have dropped the whole thing and apologized to Vashti when he was sober. But he had raved so loudly that many in the garden of the palace heard him. Since the position of women was one of total submission, the least of the King's subjects had defied him. And now it was known to the public. The prestige and power of the King for the future had suffered a serious blow.

The feast ended abruptly and on a sour note. Except for the King's officials, the people were hurried through the decorated colonnades, goblets jerked from their hands before they were emptied, and the gates of the palace garden shut behind them.

It was, of course, the kind of happening that lends itself to much talk. First it was retold for its humorous and human interest qualities. But as the days passed, political implications and rumor were added. "Xerxes, with an army of millions, had not been able to defeat a few thousand Greeks during the first years of his reign," some bitterly recalled. "And little wonder, since he can't even control his own household," others quickly added. "Perhaps Artaxerxes, the King's younger brother should be King. Was he not the stronger man? Was it not Artaxerxes, who in the war with the Greeks, had commanded the Phoenician fleet and saved it from complete destruction at the battle of Salamis after Xerxes had sailed away, thinking only of his own safety?"

These were some of the comments which Xerxes' secret agents heard in the streets. These gaushaka, called the eyes and ears of the King, had been scattered throughout the provinces and cities by Darius. For although Darius was a wise and good ruler, he knew that his control over the people rested upon fear and force, and not upon love. A King must, therefore, have a thousand eyes looking and as many ears listening to alert him as to who was planning his, or his Kingdom's, destruction.

When Xerxes' agents reported what they had heard, he knew that something had to be done. He called his seven chief advisers together and put before them a question which they no doubt dreaded answering for fear their answer would enrage the King. "In accordance with the law what is to be done to Queen

Vashti for refusing to obey a command of the King?" Xerxes asked.

After some hesitation one of the wiser of the advisers named Memucan dared put forth an answer which he felt removed the question from individuals and made it a problem of imperial importance. "Not only to the King has Queen Vashti done wrong," he began, "but to all the princes and all the men in your Kingdom. When the women of the Kingdom hear of this deed of Vashti, they will look with contempt upon their own husbands. And if they hear that no punishment came to the Queen, in harems and homes everywhere there will be contempt, disobedience, and revolt. Men will become carriers of water from the city well, and planters and reapers of onions and cucumbers in the fields."

"But what's to be done?" interrupted the King.

"If it pleases the King," Memucan continued, "let a royal order go out to all the peoples of the empire that Vashti no longer is Queen, that her crown, her jewels, and her attendants are taken from her. That the King shall choose another Queen from among the most beautiful young women of the Kingdom, one who will honor Xerxes as the King of Kings and be obedient to his commands."

Memucan's advice pleased the King and the chief princes who were assembled with him. Swift couriers carried the royal order to all the provinces. And Xerxes added to Memucan's proposal this postscript: "Let every man be lord in his own house."

To the hundred and twenty-seven provinces of the

empire Xerxes sent officials to conduct local carnivals, fairs, and contests, and bring the beauty queens of each to Susa. By this means there were brought to the Queen's palace maidens with varied backgrounds from the Indus River valley to the mountain pastures of Ethiopia, speaking different languages. It was therefore necessary for Hegai, the keeper of the Queen's palace, to conduct a school of language, manners, and customs of the court for a whole year before the maidens were ready to be presented to the King.

Soon all the provinces had supplied a candidate for the honor except the province of Susiana, the province in which the city of Susa was located. Most of the beautiful maidens of Susiana had been picked to be attendants in the court of Vashti. Now they had been sent away with the Queen. But the King had demanded that one maiden from each province be chosen. Hegai, with a hundred and twenty-six candidates and the teachers assembled for the court school, urged his agents, "Find the most beautiful maiden in the province of Susiana."

Hegai and Mordecai, however, still found time to look at any especially fine gems which came to the shop of the King's appraiser. Mordecai expressed fear that the new Queen might be more difficult to please than Vashti had been. So he and Hegai laid away many fine jewels to hold in reserve for the new Queen.

It was the custom of the Persians that a new Queen be fitted with a new crown. So on one of his visits to Mordecai, Hegai brought Vashti's crown to be melted down for remolding. He also brought all the jewels which bore Vashti's monogram or likeness. They, too, would be refaced or reinscribed by Mordecai's craftsmen when the new Queen had been chosen.

On the day that Hegai brought the jewel casket containing this dazzling display of splendor, Esther was in the front of the shop with Mordecai. When Hegai lifted the lid of the casket and began to lay the jewels before Mordecai, Esther, in an instant of exultation at seeing the Queen's crown, forgot the custom of women and raised her veil to get a better look.

Hegai stared in disbelief. Here before him was the most beautiful face he had ever seen. Motionless for a space of breathlessness, he exhaled with a shout that startled both Esther and Mordecai. "It is finished! It is finished!" he shouted, banging shut the lid of the jewel casket. Esther dropped her veil and turned away. Mordecai moved a step away from Hegai, for Hegai had thrown both his arms wide. "The King's demands are fulfilled. I need no longer fear for my place in his household." Hegai clapped his hands together and raised them above his head and began to sway back and forth, a tribal custom from the past, expressing thanks to his gods for he was a Nubian.*

"What is it? What is it that is finished, my friend?" Mordecai pleaded. "The search for the maiden in the province of Susiana who is beautiful enough to become the Queen is ended—is ended," Hegai was almost chanting, still holding his arms heavenward, still swaying. "She is here, she is here," Hegai repeated as he became suddenly calmed. "Behind Esther's veil —eyes deep and mysterious, filled with heaven's light, like mountain pools. Lips molded like a Queen's cameo out of the reddest ruby dug from the Tana highlands. Skin with the soft glow of an olive bloom just opening. Esther, your ward, the child of your heart whose beauty has surpassed the perfect grace and faith in

* The Nubians were black men from the Nile River region south of the Fifth Catarach. The men were in great demand as court slaves and attendants because of their honesty. The women were in great demand by slave traders because of their beauty and the coolness of their skin to the touch. The Nubians were not always slaves either. They ruled Egypt as Pharaohs eight hundred years before Christ. The most famous of their Pharaohs being Piankhi. Jeremiah's friend Ebed-melech was a Nubian.

which you nurtured her and brought her to womanhood."

"Stop! stop! wait. You mean Esther?" was all Mordecai could say.

Esther remained statuelike. If any words formed they were not uttered. Were her thoughts of the little girl to whom Mordecai had explained that she could not go into the Street of the Sacred Band because it was for the high persons in the King's household? Did she enjoy an instant vision of Esther, Esther herself, being the real live Queen, passing along the restricted street in her carriage with its gold-inlaid wheels, dazzling the eyes of young and old, crowded at the end of the Street of Awnings to see the Queen pass, as the child Esther had done so many times, pulling Mordecai by the hand to get to the front of the crowd?

Hegai's early excitement was now taken up by Mordecai. He began to express in a high-pitched whisper —dreams and doubts, "I would be elevated to a higher place. But Xerxes is an impetuous King, not a Cyrus or a Darius. How will he treat my child?"

Esther interrupted Mordecai. "Surely I will not be chosen Queen from among the many. But if I learn well the ways of the Queen's court, perhaps I would be kept as one of the Queen's attendants. And even tomorrow Hegai might return and say that one of my people cannot contest for the highest place in the court?"

"He will not make known your people or your kindred." Mordecai now spoke with great seriousness. "And you will never make it known. Not that I fear the King for this, because from Cyrus on, the Kings have honored us. But there are many in his household who look upon us with envy and bitterness because we have survived and prospered."

"Fear nothing," Hegai assured Mordecai. "There will be no difficulty. Already assembled are maidens of as much diversity as the many peoples of the Kingdom. There is Lydian, Egyptian, Bactrian, Nubian, Syrian, Armenian, Ethiopian, as well as Mede and Persian. And as you wish—Esther is Persian from the province of Susiana."

"But she will be gone from me," Mordecai said.

"The King's jewel appraiser and judge walks freely in the Queen's court. She will see you as you wish from the palace windows," Hegai assured Mordecai. "It is settled. Tomorrow public proclamation will be made that the contest in the province of Susiana is ended. I will send a carriage to bring you to the house of the Queen's attendants. At the gate of the palace I shall have seven of the best servants waiting to serve Esther. And daily my friend Mordecai shall walk in the garden of the court, at our chosen hour, to learn from Esther herself how well she fares. I will keep secret that which you wish. You keep secret the fact that the former Queen's jewels are in your shop lest robbers come and leave the future Queen crownless and jeweless."

The next day Esther entered the Queen's palace according to Hegai's plan. Mordecai's misgivings about Esther's going to the palace disappeared as he went to the Queen's garden day after day. He felt an inward grace and warmth as he saw his ward walking regally, attended by her servants.

She described to Mordecai the exotic foods spread for them in the Queen's house. She had Mordecai feel the texture of the fine garments she wore, and told him of the sweet ointments and warm baths in goat's milk.

Esther found the training very easy. She already knew the language and the history of the land, an advantage over many of the maidens who came from remote provinces.

"You must remember well the history of the Persians which you recited to me at our lessons," Mordecai reminded her as they talked from time to time. "I taught you the history of our people, the faith of Abraham, the glorious deeds of Moses and David, the thoughts and sayings of the prophets, and the Mezuzah which says 'the Lord shall perserve thy going out and thy coming in from this time forth, even for evermore.' But when you are called before Xerxes, you must remember the deeds of the Persians: Cyrus, Cambyses, and Darius. You must remember the thoughts of Zoroaster, the great prophet of the Persians."

Esther heeded the words of Mordecai and grew in wisdom and in beauty. On his frequent visits to Mordecai's shop Hegai assured the old man that Esther was wiser and more beautiful than the rest. "The King already favors her with gifts," he said.

"But will this not stir up jealousy among the maidens?" Mordecai asked. "Will they not one day discover our secret and send word to Xerxes 'Esther is a Jewess'?"

"Have no fear," Hegai spoke with glee. "The time approaches when the King will choose his Queen. On that day I will come with the measurement of the circle of the Queen's head. And that measurement will be the size to rest lightly upon Esther's temple. Then you will not trust your craftsmen. With your own hands you will shape the gold. You will pick each gem for rarity, and inlay each with your own fingers. You and the King will be equally happy on that day. So you will be as happy as a King. And I will know the happiness of one who discovered a Queen."

Thus passed the weeks and months until the time of choosing drew near. Then in the tenth month of the maidens' training all that Hegai had predicted came to pass. Xerxes chose Esther for his Queen in the seventh year of his reign.

As Hegai had said, Mordecai shaped the Queen's crown with his own hands. Hegai chose wisely from among the maidens for attendants to wait upon the Queen and sent the rest back to the provinces. At the same time there went out a royal proclamation that Esther was the Queen of the hundred and twenty-seven provinces, that all princes and peoples would henceforth honor her.

How proud Mordecai was at the coronation. He saw the jeweled crown of his own making placed upon Esther's head. He moved among princes and officials

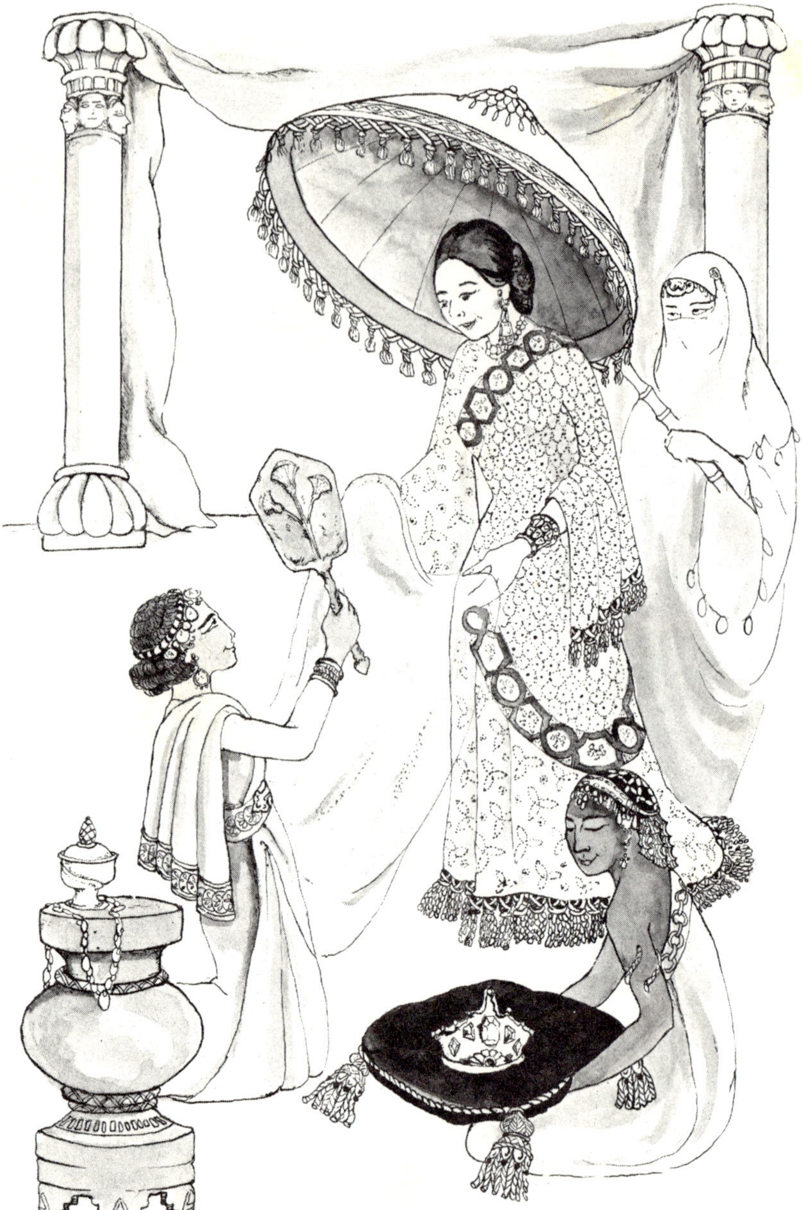

in the great Hall of a Hundred Columns. His heart warmed within him as he watched Esther walk its long length between lines of princes and bow before the King. When the King took her hand and directed her to the throne seat beside him, Mordecai raised his hand and wiped tears of joy from where they had trickled into his beard.

3

Mordecai did not go to the palace garden now to meet the Queen as he had gone when his beloved Esther was only a member of the Queen's household. He knew that there were officials in the court who knew he was a Jew, and if they learned that he was Esther's guardian, they might in jealousy and bitterness expose her. Then they would spread word in the streets: "Xerxes, a Persian, one of a people whose power and empire is the envy of the Gods, with the whole world to choose from, has made a Jewess his Queen. One of a people who have been slaves to Egypt, the Egypt which Persia has conquered. Now the Jews live among us as foreigners. Why do we have a foreigner for a Queen?"

This Mordecai did not wish to happen. It would cause trouble for Esther and for Xerxes. So Mordecai contented himself to sit often near the Gate of the Golden Spearmen and hear the talk of the court, or pass through the service gate (the Needle's Eye) which was his right. From there he could glance up and Esther could wave to him from the palace windows, for Hegai came often to the shop, bringing cheerful messages from the Queen, and telling Mordecai when Esther would be sitting by her window. For Hegai, too, loved Esther. As chief custodian of the Queen's household he knew that if a Queen's demands were not met, she could point her finger and he would be executed. But Esther demanded little. In her presence Hegai felt as though he served a friend. She made him forget that he was a slave.

One day when Hegai arrived at Mordecai's shop, he found Mordecai in a great state of excitement. "Get word to Esther, so she can warn the King, that the King's life is in danger," Mordecai began as he guided Hegai outside so the workers in the shop would not hear. "As I sat by the Gate of the Golden Spearmen I heard two men plotting to murder the King so that Artaxerxes could rule in his stead. They are a part of the King's outer guard, the night watch at the threshold of the Hall of Columns. I did not know them, but when they left I asked the captain of the gate who they were. He told me where they guard and their names. They are Bigthan and Teresh, Bactrians both, and Artaxerxes lives there in Ecbatana."

"Brother has murdered brother for kingdoms before. Cambyses murdered—" but Hegai did not have a chance to finish.

"Go now, go quickly. Tell Esther they plan to murder the King in his night chambers. It could be this very night. Tell her to send word even before the

King dines." Mordecai had been tugging Hegai toward the Needle's Eye as he spoke.

Hegai clasped his hand and said, "You have no doubt?"

"It is certain," Mordecai replied. "Tell Esther to hurry." And he pushed Hegai gently toward the gate.

All that Mordecai had said was true. Esther sent a message, sealed with the Queen's seal, to warn Xerxes. This was her message: "Hegai heard from Mordecai, the Queen's jewel appraiser, that Bigthan and Teresh, who guard the threshold of the Hall of Columns, plan evil against the King—to murder him. Mordecai heard this from their own lips as he sat by the Gate of the Golden Spearmen."

Esther could not carry the message herself. The Queen could not go to the King's palace except when he sent for her. Anyone, even the Queen, who entered the great throne room without being called by the King, was executed unless the King held out his scepter that they might touch it.

When Esther's message came to the King, a watch was set over Bigthan and Teresh. During the night watch they admitted four confederates past the threshold door of the Hall of Columns. They, along with Bigthan and Teresh were seized and hanged by the city gates—a warning to all who would plot against the King.†

---

† Fourteen years later Xerxes was murdered in his night chambers by a palace guard named Artabanus, hired by Artaxerxes who became King.

Mordecai had saved the King's life. After the hours of public hanging were ended for those executed (the corpses hung for a day and a night), Hegai came hurriedly to Mordecai's shop. He could not come sooner. The law forbade passage in or out the palace gates until all danger was ended, and all who "plotted dark deeds had seen the naked corpses bleaching" in the sun.

"The name of Mordecai has been proclaimed throughout the palaces as first citizen of the Kingdom." Hegai spoke with boastful pride to his friend. "You saved the King's life. The deed is recorded in the Book of Chronicles of the King. The scroll was hung in the Hall of Columns and in the Queen's palace for all to read. Great honor will come to you. It is rumored in the palace that the King will not promote his friend Haman, the Arab of the Amalekites, to the position of grand vizier, the office next to that of the King himself. Many say that Mordecai, who has aided the King's treasury by wise appraisals and weighing, who saved the King's life, will be appointed. Esther smiles with silent pride as she listens to the rumors. But she says nothing."

"You should be the grand vizier, Hegai," Mordecai jested as he put his hand on his friend's shoulder. "Indeed you should be King. You would give the Kingdom over to your friends and rumor would replace law."

"You jest unwisely, Mordecai. Rumor often influences and replaces decree and law. Rumor is against Haman. It is said in the palace that the King would choose Haman for his wealth, not for his courage. The story goes the rounds that against the Greek at the Battle of Mt. Mycale, in Asia Minor, Haman and his Arabs ran away and left the Phoenicians under the command of Tigranes, Xerxes' cousin, to suffer terrible defeat at the hands of Xanthippius the Greek."

"Hegai, I do not know of what you speak. But I do believe you feed upon rumor, my friend. As for me, I am happy to live quietly as the King's jewel appraiser. Who knows but that the King will have second thoughts and lay suspicion on Mordecai. Suppose he sent for me and asked, 'Mordecai, is the King's life only worthy of a third-hand message? Why did you not warn me directly?' He could torture me. And I would die not giving away Esther's secret."

"No more, Mordecai. You look on the dark side. You will be honored," Hegai reassured his friend.

"I beg you, Hegai, do not link my name with rumors for appointment to any office, especially one that has to do with Haman, the Arab of the Amalekites. You do not know the history of my people. For as many generations as separate me from Moses, the Amalekite and Jew have been traditional enemies. And legend carries it back to Abraham. The story tells how they and their kindred tribesmen, the Elamites, filled the water holes of Negeb with earth so that Abraham and his flocks would perish from the earth. They contested the land with Joshua, with Saul, with David, and marched with Necho, the Egyptian, against Josiah at Megiddo. There they slew Josiah, our young and noble King who had purified the law and the temple."

"Your fears are of yesteryear, Mordecai, when peoples and nations were divided. Now they are united under Xerxes. Haman serves Xerxes, the King of Kings, not his tribesmen. Have no fear. Accept the honor that will come to you. I go now, but will come soon to escort you to the palace."

"You did not come for a rare gem from the caravans for the King to give Esther? Is it not the custom that whenever she is called, he gives her a gift? He has not commissioned one for many days. Is all well with Esther, the Queen?" Mordecai asked.

"All is well with your child, the Queen. It is a big empire, Mordecai. The King has to remember more than which of his hundred robes to wear. He has a thousand things to vex and trouble him. Right now its probably taxes and his young brother, Artaxerxes. Again, I go now, before the Needle's Eye is barred for the night. There is still an air of nervous caution in the palace grounds. I'll come soon—with news."

When Hegai returned to the palace, Mordecai dismissed from his mind all thought of honor and promotion. He watched for the relaxing of security at the palace gate. When the special guards were removed, he again walked in the garden at the appointed hour and waved to Esther.

It was not long before Haman's promotion to grand vizier became known. Hegai still speculated that Mordecai would be honored. He also tried to explain Haman's appointment in a way that would please his friend, saying, "It was for his wealth. Haman is very rich. He is also very clever, clever enough to turn truth to lie and make it sound like truth. He knows how to flatter the King, and his court manner is most pleasing. But for all that he is a proud and overbearing man."

"And is worse since his promotion," Mordecai began. "He has reissued a decree that has not been enforced since Nebuchadnezzar, except for a brief period under Darius. He has decreed in the King's name that when a chariot bearing the King's insignia passes, all men must bow down. His chariot bears the insignia. Morning and evening he passes on the Street of the Sacred Band. All the people except me, at the entrance to the Street of Awnings, bow before his chariot. Already he has slowed his gold-bridled horses and stared at me."

"But why do you not bow, Mordecai?" Hegai asked, and added, "It is not in you to be envious, and besides, the King must certainly have in store for you some other honor."

"You do not understand, Hegai. I am not envious.

Your dream of honor for Mordecai amuses me. I do not bow down to Haman, or any man, because the commandment of the one true God, the God of my people, says that we shall bow to Him only. Do you know the story of Shadrach, Meshach, and Abednego? They would not bow to the ninety-foot statue of Nebuchadnezzar that he had built on the Plain of Dura.

"They had been promoted to offices in Nebuchadnezzar's Kingdom, and envious people, perhaps Amalekites, reported them. Nebuchadnezzar called them in and said—"

"Wait," Hegai interrupted. "Here comes Haman's chariot now. Go into the shop. I will bow. I came into Persia a slave, led by a rope with a ring in my nose. My tribal gods do not object to my being a slave for a foolish ritual in order that I may be free to walk fetterless for all my days."

Hegai bowed with all the rest of the people in the bazaar except Mordecai. Mordecai stood erect, watching the sky. He did not see Haman tap his driver on the shoulder, or the driver draw upon the reins to slow the chariot.

"Do not look so troubled," Mordecai said to Hegai, when the chariot had passed. "I was telling you the story of Shadrach, Meshach, and Abednego.

"Nebuchadnezzar called them in and said, 'Is it true that you do not bow to the image which I set up? If you do not I must keep the law and cast you into the bowels of the iron likeness of Marduk, the chief god of Babylon, which is the furnace where

44

we offer sacrifice to appease Marduk. Who is the god who can save you then?'

"Then they answered, 'If our God whom we serve is able to deliver us, He will deliver us from the burning fiery furnace. But if not, it is important for you to know, O King, that we will not bow down to your image or serve your gods.'

"Nebuchadnezzar did not know the last remark was a testimony of their faith which even death in a fiery furnace would not shake. He thought they were defiant and arrogant, so he had them thrown into the furnace. He was so mad that he ordered the furnace to be heated seven times hotter than when four Babylonian youths were sacrificed to Marduk at the Planting Festival."

"What a way to die," Hegai interrupted, and added, "laws are more rigid in the destruction of those who disobey than in the protection of those who keep them."

"But Shadrach, Meshach, and Abednego were not destroyed," Mordecai continued. "The one true God would not let the flames of Marduk touch them. When Nebuchadnezzar opened the furnace door after the fire died down, there they stood in the center of the furnace, singing a hymn to their God.

"Nebuchadnezzar was so surprised that he cried out, 'Blessed be the God of Shadrach, Meshach, and Abednego.' Then he issued a decree which said: 'Any people, nation, or language that speaks anything against the God of Shadrach, Meshach, and Abednego shall be torn limb from limb, and their houses laid in ruins.'

"Then the King executed those who had reported Shadrach, Meshach, and Abednego because he feared their god might bring punishment upon him. And he promoted the three to higher places in his Kingdom.

"So you see, Hegai, their God, who is my God, can deliver me from Haman's wrath. But if not, I will still not bow down to him."

Hegai rose to go but did not speak.

"Wait, I have another story. It is the story of Daniel and the King to whom he would not pray."

"Some other time. I must go." Hegai spoke in a low voice as he backed around the corner of the shop. "I see two of Haman's bodyguards at the end of the street. They are pointing this way and conversing with those who loiter by the gate."

Some who sat daily by the gate had asked Mordecai why he alone did not bow down and do obeisance to Haman. He had replied openly, "I am a Jew and bow only to the one true God of Israel."

After that some spoke sympathetically to Mordecai, saying, "Dare you disobey the King's command?" Others mocked him loudly as Haman passed, saying, "Bow down your face to the dust old gray-hair."

These who mocked had been nothing less than happy to tell Haman's bodyguards that Mordecai was a Jew. "He is above Haman's law," they laughingly informed the bodyguards. "He has a God and to Him only he bows and obeys."

When word came to Haman that the defiant old gray-hair who stood in the Street of Awnings or at the gate of the city was a Jew named Mordecai, the hate fuel of all the years of enmity between Amalekites and the Jews burned with a great fury in his heart.

"Mordecai, the Jew, refuses to obey a royal decree. He must die," Haman announced to his assembled attendants as he walked up and down in the court of his house, grinding his teeth.

Now there was among his advisers a wise man who had seen service in the court of Darius, the King. When Haman's temper had cooled, the wise one said to him, "In the court of Darius there was an appointed prince, a Jew named Daniel. When other princes sought to destroy him, they themselves were executed."

"Tell me the story. What has it to do with me?" Haman demanded in anger.

"The memory prompted me," the wise man replied. "I think Daniel had disobeyed a royal decree. The Jews are a people apart. They have laws of their own which they call commandments; these they put above all other law."

"Do not tell me of the Jews, those robbers of the pastures of my forefathers and my fathers. But what of Daniel?" Haman asked a second time.

"The memory that prompted me fails," the wise one began, "but there is in your Counting House a lesser scribe, an old man who is a Jew. His name is Shekthar, which means counter of coins. He will know the details of the story of Daniel. For it is a principle peculiar to the Jews to know all the deeds and the history of their people."

"Are you a Jew? You speak as one—in veiled praise. Bring the Jew Shekthar from the Counting House," Haman commanded in anger.

The scribe was hastened into the presence of Haman. "Tell me the story of Daniel, the Jew," Haman ordered.

The aged scribe pulled the bend of years out of his back and stood erect. His eyes brightened and he began, announcing a title which was different from Haman's, "The Story of Daniel, the Prince." Then he went quickly through the story. "When Darius became King he chose a hundred and twenty princes to rule the provinces which then made up the Kingdom. Over the princes he set three chief advisers. Now the first of these was Daniel, whose wisdom Darius had had made known to him from the days of Belshazzar. For Daniel was an interpreter of dreams. When Darius heard that Daniel had foretold the fall of Babylon, he made him the first adviser. This made Daniel the most highly honored man in the Kingdom except the King himself."

"What happened? Get to the heart of the story," Haman demanded.

"A bitter jealousy began to possess the princes and the other two chief advisers. They watched him carefully to discover some fault or act of faithlessness that might displease the King. They found nothing. But in their close watching they became aware that three times a day Daniel knelt by his window with his face turned toward Jerusalem and prayed. When they learned further of Daniel's faith in his God, they hit upon an idea to destroy him.

"Now at this time Darius' popularity with the people was very low. He had suffered great casualties and a humiliating defeat at the hands of the Scythians, a barbarous people in the North, against whom he should never have marched."

"What has this to do with Daniel?" Haman screamed and jumped from his dais, shaking his finger right before Shekthar's eyes. "If you can't make the story shorter I'll cut off half your tongue."

Shekthar continued without a change of pace or voice. "The King's unpopularity gave those who wanted to destroy Daniel an idea. They went to Darius and suggested an Honor the King month. During that month the King would be honored as a god, and all men would pray to the King only and bow down to him.

"The royal decree was published throughout the Kingdom and this was its wording: 'Whoever shall ask a request of any god or man for thirty days, except of Darius, the King of Kings, shall be cast into a den of lions.' Daniel heard about it. But three times every day Daniel continued to kneel by his window with his face toward Jerusalem and pray aloud to his God, the God of Abraham and Moses.

"Daniel's enemies were quick to report him to Darius. 'This exile from Judah, Daniel, in whom you have placed trust, pays no heed to your decree.'

"Now Darius respected Daniel for his wisdom and his service. He cared not that Daniel was a foreigner and exile. Most of Darius' princes were foreigners one to another. He would have saved Daniel, but the envious princes clamored so loud that Darius ordered Daniel to be brought and cast into the lions' den.

"Just before Daniel was led away, the King came near him and whispered, 'May the God whom you serve so faithfully deliver you from the lions.'

"Then the King went away hurriedly to the palace. All that night the King tossed upon his couch or walked up and down in his night chambers. His servants brought him wine to drink but he sent them away. When the first light of dawn broke over the towers of the city, Darius called his guards and went on foot through the silent streets to the lions' den. He listened at the stone door. Then in an anguished voice called out, 'O Daniel, servant of the living God, has your God, whom you serve so faithfully, been able to save you from the lions?'

"No sound of the great cats growling and fighting came out to Darius. Had they devoured their prey and stretched themselves in contented sleep as was their jungle habit? Darius wondered.

"His attendants did not understand their King's strange behavior. They had seen traitors go to the lions' den before. They stood in puzzled silence, wondering why the King was so concerned."

Haman had ceased his ranting, and was enveloped in deep thought. A scowl replacing his wrinkled forehead, he signaled Shekthar that he had better relieve the suspense, and get to the end of the story. So he continued.

"Then a quiet voice came from within, 'O King, live forever. I was found blameless before my Lord; and also before you. He shut the mouths of the lions.

O King, I have done no wrong.'

"Darius ordered the door opened, and while his attendants stood with spears fixed, lest the lions escape, Daniel walked calmly from the den.

"When Darius had rejoiced for the safety of Daniel, he quickly turned his wrath upon the leaders who had conspired to get rid of the adviser of whom they were jealous. The chief conspirators were thrown to the lions. Daniel's God did not close the lions' mouths for them. Those who would have destroyed Daniel were themselves destroyed. And Daniel received honors and prospered mightily.

"Darius even issued a decree that: 'All men shall tremble and fear before the God of Daniel. He delivers and rescues, He works signs and wonders.'"

Haman sat in troubled silence. His wise counselor feared that a sudden outburst of anger might bring harm to Shekthar. For Shekthar had told much that Haman perhaps wished he had not heard. So the counselor motioned Shekthar from the chambers.

Haman's pride and anger did not let him remain silent long. He began to laugh with a mad laughter and spoke: "A number of princes conspiring to rid the Kingdom of one Jew! Who could question Darius' wrath against them? Theirs was a cowardly act. But what would a King do for a single prince who dared rid his Kingdom of all the Jews and gave their property into his treasury? The King would honor that man."

Haman asked no more advice of his advisers. But those who had remained quiet heartily approved in chorus, "Brave words, O Visier." The wise one who had spoken out now held his peace.

4

The ancient enmity between Haman's tribe and the Jews stirred Haman to a plan which made him both excited and gleeful. He would not belittle his princely position by "punishing one gray-haired Jew." He would destroy them all throughout the whole Kingdom. And he was convinced that his plan would work.

Now Haman knew that Xerxes did not know by name and custom all the many peoples that made up his empire. Since he became King, he had spent most of his time putting down a revolt in Egypt and directing an expedition against the Greeks.

So when Haman went to the King with his plan to destroy the Jews, he was sufficiently general in his description that Xerxes might well have thought he was describing Egyptians or Greeks.

Haman made the following proposal: "There is a certain people scattered abroad and dispersed among the peoples in all the provinces of your Kingdom. Their laws are different from those of every other people (now this would have certainly applied to the Greeks) and they do not keep the King's law, so that it is not for the King's profit to tolerate them. If it please the King, let it be decreed that they be destroyed and their property taken away."

Haman further explained to Xerxes that he would advance the pay of those hired to carry out the extermination program. It would be at no cost to the King, but the King would get vast sums poured into his treasury from the property that these greedy and lawless people had accumulated in his Kingdom.

Xerxes, as we have already seen, was quick tempered and inclined to act without thinking. He believed Haman, and without even asking who these people were, flew into a rage and called a scribe to write the proclamation:

"Having become ruler of many nations and master of the whole world, I have determined to settle the lives of my subjects in lasting tranquillity.

"When I asked my counselors how this might be accomplished, Haman, who excels among us in sound judgment, and is distinguished for his unchanging good will and steadfast honesty, and is second in command in the Kingdom, has pointed out that within the Kingdom there is scattered a hostile people who have laws contrary to those of every nation, and disregard the ordinances of the King. Their opposition is such that our Kingdom cannot attain stability. Therefore, I have decreed that those indicated to you in the letters of Haman, shall all, with their wives and children, be utterly destroyed by the sword, without pity or mercy."

All that Haman had designed, in bitterness and

53

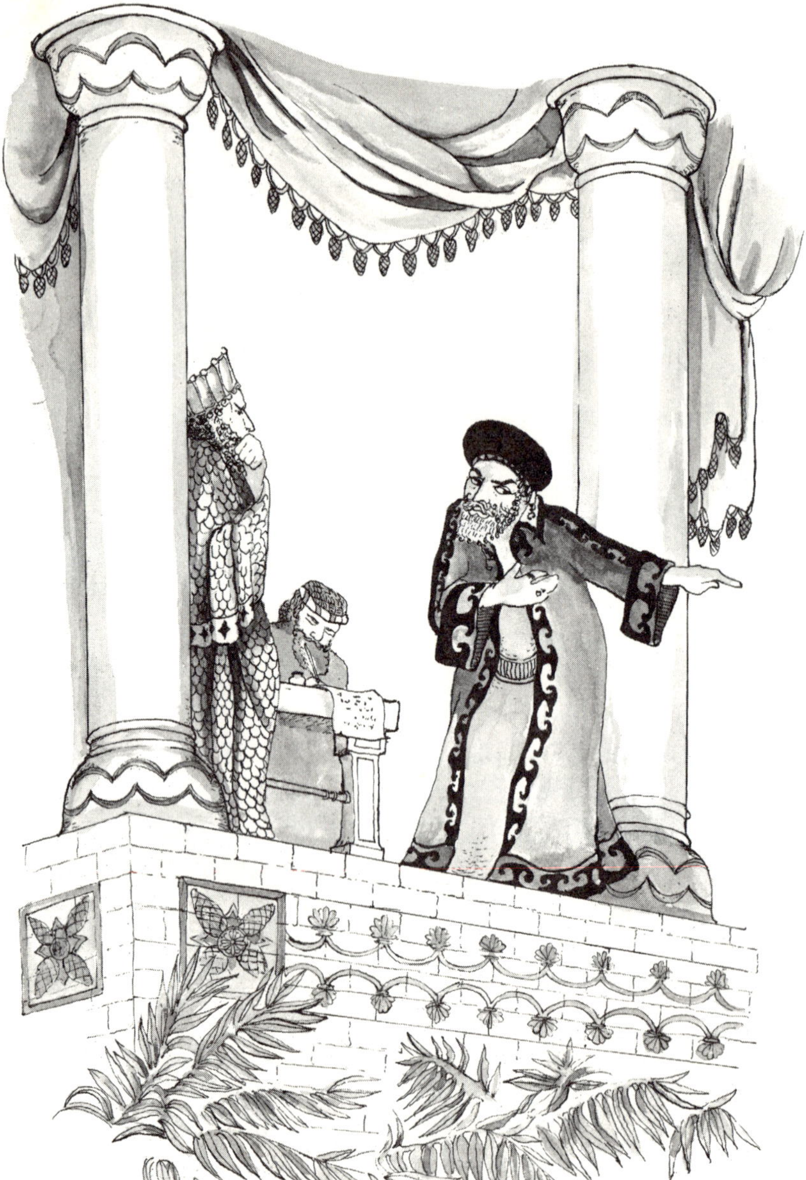

hatred, was now perfected. He, of course, could seal orders with the stamp of the King's signet ring, so the King would never see the people named for extermination. Haman and Xerxes sat down and drank to Haman's sound judgment and the King's concern for peace and stability throughout his whole vast lands.

Haman was determined to further impress the King. So he prepared his letters designating that the whole plan would be carried out in one day. The order which went by Persia's fast couriers to every corner of the empire carried this grim message: "Destroy, slay, annihilate all Jews, young and old, women and children, in one day, the thirteenth day of Adar (February), and plunder their goods."

This would have been Haman's perfect day except for one thing. When his chariot passed the Gate of the Golden Spearmen as he left the palace grounds all the people bowed low. All save one. He stood erect, not even turning his eyes, with the many curious or admiring, to look at the chariot, flashing only a little less gold decoration than that of the King's royal chariot.

The contents of Haman's order of doom became known quickly in the streets of Susa. The puzzlement of it was almost equal to the distress it brought to young and old. "Why?" was the single word which passed from lip to lip. With thoughts of past oppression and the kindness Cyrus had shown, the achievement of high places such as Daniel had known because of the wisdom, peace, and honor which they had demonstrated by their lives in the Kingdom, they reasoned among themselves. Their reasoning brought no answer. Only the repeated "Why?" as they looked at their young and concealed their silent tears.

They had worked at honest toil for the prosperity they enjoyed. They had lived where they had been told to live. Though far from Jerusalem and the holy temple, they had prayed three times a day with their eyes toward the city of their one true God. Now they were to be destroyed and their property seized for the King's treasury.

When they found no answer as to the reason for the decree, far more cruel than slavery in Egypt or captivity in Babylon, their silence gave way to cries of agony. They put on sackcloth and sat in ashes, their ancient custom for mourning. They fasted on unleavened bread and water, and prayed day and night without ceasing. They stared with hopeless eyes at the walls of the palace from which the decree had come. They longed for a prophet, a Jeremiah or a Daniel, to speak, to stand before the King.

Mordecai's grief was greater than that of any other. He knew at once that Haman's bodyguards, who had seen Hegai with him in the Street of Awnings, had asked Hegai why he came often to the Jew's shop. Hegai, fearful that Esther's secret might be found out, had agreed with Mordecai that they must not be seen together.

Mordecai knew that Esther would die too. Surely she would be found out. And his friend Hegai would die because he had brought Esther to the palace and had kept her secret. Now Mordecai mourned in sackcloth and ashes. He could no longer pass through the palace gate to wave to Esther because no one in mourning was considered ritually clean.

Inside the Queen's palace Haman's decree had not become known. It was Hegai who had always brought news to the Queen. Now Hegai had not been in the streets for many days.

Esther watched day after day for Mordecai to walk in the garden so she could wave to him. Finally she sent Hathach, a Jew himself, whom Hegai had assigned as her messenger, into the street to see if all was well with Mordecai.

Hathach found Mordecai mourning with his people. When Mordecai had told him all that had happened, he gave Hathach a copy of Haman's decree to carry to Esther in secret. He also gave Hathach this message for the Queen: "You only can speak to the King. Go to him and tell him that an innocent people are to be murdered, among them many who serve his court faithfully. But Haman has marked them for death because they also serve their one true God faithfully."

When Esther received the decree of Haman and Mordecai's message, she felt both grief and guilt. All night she tossed sleepless upon her silken couch. Her servants bathed her in warm milk and rubbed her with sweet ointments, but the pain was in her heart. She thought of rushing from the palace to comfort Mordecai. But this the Queen could not do. She wished she had never become the Queen at all.

She thought she would send word to Mordecai to hide and save himself, that she herself would be safe inside the palace.

But when morning came she knew she could not belittle Mordecai's character by asking him to become a coward. So she wrote this message and sent Hathach to deliver it to Mordecai: "There is a law of the Persians which is unlike the law of the Jews. The law of the Jews, when the Jews had a King, as you taught me, allowed whoever had been wronged to enter the court and proclaim evil. You told me of Elijah who stood before Ahab and told him to his face that the one true God of the Jews would punish him because he had murdered Naboth for his vineyard. You told me how Nathan entered David's court and denounced him to his face for having Uriah, the Hittite, killed in the front of battle, so David could have Uriah's wife, Bath-sheba, for his own.

"But the law of the Persian decrees certain death for anyone who enters the King's chambers without being called. The King sits on his throne with his scepter in his hand. If he holds it out for the one who has entered uncalled to touch, that one lives. If he does not extend his scepter, then the one who has come uninvited is put to death.

"I have not been called to come in to the King for more than thirty days now. If I go uncalled, and am no longer favored in his eyes, I will not be sent away as Vashti was, I will surely die."

When Mordecai read Esther's message, his thoughts dwelt long upon the homeland from which his people had come. He thought of David, the King, and Jerusalem, the City of David. Would it not have been better for him to have taken his young ward, the child Esther, and returned to the land which the one true God had given Abraham for the Jews?

"But if the living God raised up Shadrach, Meshach, Abednego, and Daniel in the land of their captivity to serve their people, might He not also raise up Esther?" Mordecai asked himself.

So he wrote Esther this message: "Think not that in the King's palace you will escape any more than all the other Jews. And who knows whether you have not been raised up and come to the Kingdom for such a time as this?"

Esther read Mordecai's message, and for it she could find no easy answer. Could she deny faith in the one true God and all that Mordecai had taught her by still letting fear keep her from going before the King? Had God permitted her to become Queen so that she might save her people? As she reread Mordecai's message she felt a deep shame. She had feared, but now the faith he had taught her made her strong.

So Hathach carried her answer to Mordecai: "Gather all the Jews in Susa that they may fast and pray for three days that God will give me favor in the eyes of the King. Neither eat nor drink, day or night, I and my maidens will also fast and pray as you do. Then I will go to the King, though it is against the law; and if I perish, I perish."

The message did not disturb Mordecai. In it he saw that Esther's faith had carried her out of the realm of fear. A certain calm came to Mordecai as he said to himself, "The King will receive Esther the Queen. But if not," Shadrach had said to Nebuchadnezzar, "the living God can save me from the fiery furnace; but if not I will still not bow down and worship other gods and your golden image."

"But if not, but if not," Mordecai repeated to himself.

So Mordecai gathered the people to fast and pray for three days, as Esther had ordered him. And as the three days had passed, Mordecai looked often toward the Queen's palace as he prayed and waited.

When the days of prayer were finished, Esther, dressed in her most somber-colored royal robes, entered the great Hall of Columns. The distance between columns seemed to get longer and longer as she walked the three hundred feet toward the door to the throne room.

The door to the throne room was open. Esther paused to still a slight trembling that was shaking the wide sleeves of her purple robe and causing her jeweled arm bracelets to tinkle. Before her sat the King on the golden throne, its legs carved to have it rest on lions' paws. Upright in his hand the gold-inlaid scepter, with its knob of pure gold capped by precious stones. It was about the height of a man so that if the King stretched it forth, one bowing before the King could easily touch it.

Esther took one last glance at the end of the scepter, which within seconds would mean life or death to her, and entered. Xerxes was so surprised

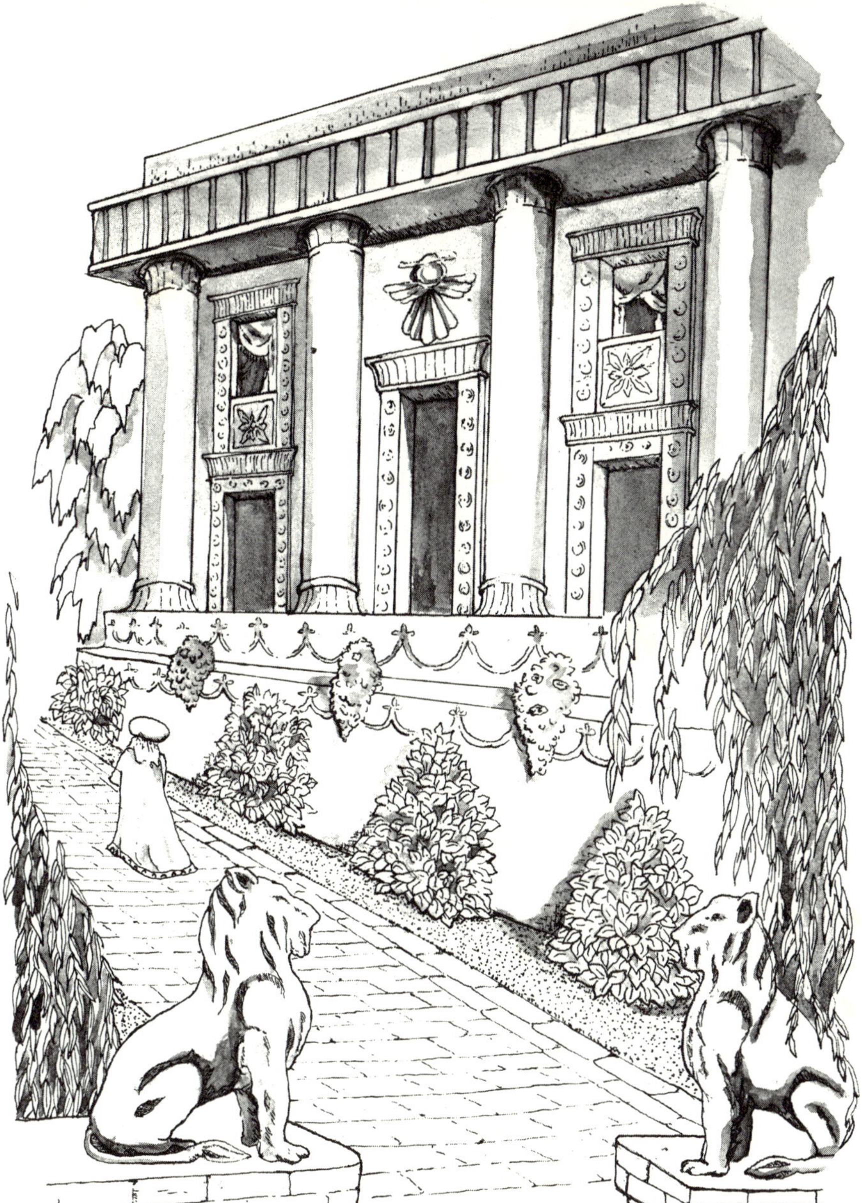

that he jerked backward, and for a moment the scepter pointed away from Esther rather than toward her. But after the instant of surprise the King leaned forward, holding the point of the scepter for Esther to touch. Sensing that something out of the ordinary had brought his Queen, now standing beautiful but silent before him, he said in a soft voice, "What is it, Queen Esther? What is your request? It shall be given to you, even to the half of my Kingdom."

Esther's wisdom and faith had prompted her to

decide before she came to the King, that if she were received agreeably she would postpone her request until she could confront Haman in the presence of the King. When the King stood up and reached for her hand, Esther's confidence was complete. She could carry out her own plan.

The King, still sensing urgency, asked again, "What is your wish, my Queen?"

And Esther's reply came as a surprise. "If it please the King," she spoke quietly, "let the King and his grand vizier, Haman, come today to dine with me at the Queen's palace."

The King was deeply touched and flattered. Affairs of the Kingdom had kept him so long from his beautiful Queen that she had risked her life to come to him unannounced. He immediately sent word to Haman. Then flanked by attendants he returned with Esther to the Queen's palace.

When Haman arrived and found that he only had been invited to dine with the King and Queen, his pride swelled within him. His arrogance whispered to him over golden goblets of wine that he could now do no wrong.

And as they were drinking wine, the King said again to Esther, "What is your request, my Queen? Even to half my Kingdom, it shall be fulfilled."

The King was so used to having people ask for big favors that he still thought Esther wanted somebody executed, more fountains in the palace garden, new beds of ivory and gold to replace the wood and gold-inlaid ones in the Queen's palace, or high offices for some newly discovered relatives in some corner of the Kingdom which was rich in gold and silver.

Again Esther surprised and pleased him. "If I have found favor in your eyes, my King, my request is that you and Haman dine with me tomorrow as you have done today. This is my great wish. Tomorrow I will tell you my greater wish."

Indeed, they would be happy to come. These two days had given the King a diversion from the weighty affairs of the Kingdom. When he left the Queen's palace, he waved his litter carriers away and walked back through the palace gardens.

Haman left in his chariot, standing erect, his princely robes fanning the breeze. Proud and gleeful, he dashed out of the palace grounds to hurry home to tell Zeresh, his wife, and his attendants that he had been invited to dine with the King and Queen again. Surely some new honor must be coming to him. And this was his thought, when, as he passed the Gate of the Golden Spearmen, his bright glee blackened into rancor.

At the sight of his chariot the people in the street bowed their faces to the earth. All save one. Mordecai stood at the gate where he had been waiting, praying, listening, hoping. Though a feeling of deep concern weighed upon him, he did not bow.

Haman was inclined to be loudly boastful, as arrogant people are. When he arrived home, he described to his wife, Zeresh, and his household how he had dined alone with the King and Queen. "And surely some special honor awaits me," he bragged, "for I am to dine with them in the Queen's palace again tomorrow." He then reviewed his many accomplishments and the splendor of his riches, all of which Zeresh and the others had heard many times before.

No wonder Zeresh, quite bored and perhaps a little jealous, was ready to belittle his self-measurement of power and greatness when he changed the subject to Mordecai.

"Yet all my power and wealth do me no good when I see the Jew Mordecai, the only man who does not bow down to me," Haman said. His mood had again changed to grimness.

"Then why don't you build a gallows fifty cubits high outside the palace wall and hang him on it?" Zeresh suggested cynically. "If you have so much favor with the King he will surely approve the execution. I have heard that on his return from Greece, when a storm came up at sea, he had half the sailors thrown overboard to lighten the ship. And when he landed safely on land, it is said he had the ship's captain and the rest of the crew murdered in order that it would not be noised in the empire that the King was a coward.

"Build the gallows, arrive early at the palace for the King's permission. He will send word of approval from his night chambers by an attendant, thinking some violence has been attempted against the person of his vizier and most favored prince."

Haman did not call his counselors. He called instead his soldiers and commanded them to conscript wagons for hauling logs and beams, and workers to hammer through the night so that the gallows would be ready at dawn. He ordered the gallows built in sight of the palace and not far from the Gate of the Golden Spearmen. On this spot the King would be able to see from his window with what prompt action his vizier carried out the law. And those who loitered by the gate would from tomorrow forth not only bow, but tremble at the sight of Haman.

While Haman's captains yelled commands, amid the clatter of wagon wheels, the thunder of rolling beams, and the sound of heaving workmen and yelling overseers, the King tossed sleepless on his soft couch,

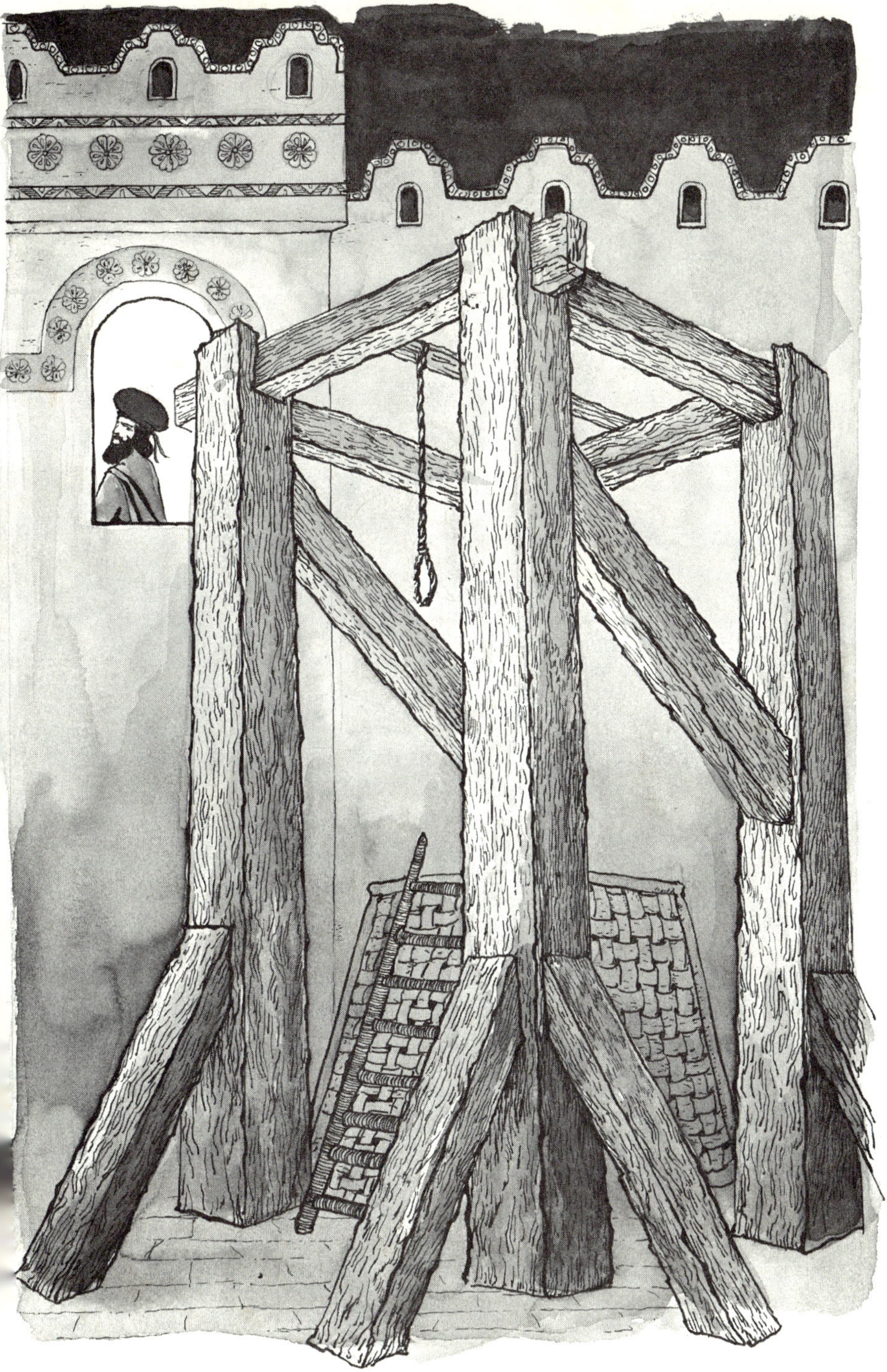

wondering why the night was unusually noisy. At last he ordered his scribe to his night chambers and had him read from the Annals of the King, the memorable Deeds of Xerxes; and all that had happened during his reign. Toward morning the scribe read the story of how Mordecai had saved the King's life by reporting the assassination plot of Bigthan and Teresh.

"What honor or dignity has been bestowed upon Mordecai for the kindness done to me? Why is it not recorded to show the King's gratitude?" the King asked half rising from his couch.

"Nothing has been done for him, O King. The palace was in turmoil for fear harm might come to the King from other plotters. Mordecai was forgotten for the moment in our anxiety," reasoned the scribe with a note of anxiety in his own voice, fearing for his own safety.

Just at that moment there was the sound of voices and footsteps in the outer chamber. Haman had finished the gallows and now that dawn was breaking, he had arrived to get the King's seal for the execution.

"Who is in the court?" the King asked of the attendant who stood in the door.

"Haman is here, standing in the outer chamber," the attendant replied.

"Let him come in," the King ordered.

Now to be invited directly into the King's night chambers was only for the very special people who surrounded the King. So Haman entered proudly, wondering what service the King was going to ask him to perform.

"Haman," the King asked, "what shall be done to a man whom the King delights to honor?"

The King had spoken before Haman had had a chance to request his execution permit. For now that could wait. "Who but me!" thought Haman. "Whom would the King make mention of honoring so early, before he is awake, except one who came into his presence? He means me!"

Believing that the King meant him, Haman answered, "For the man whom the King delights to honor, let robes like those of the King be brought, and one of the King's pure white horses, and a crown like unto that of the King. Let these be put in the hands of one of the King's most noble princes. Let the prince put the royal robe and crown on the man whom the King has chosen to honor. Let the people of the city be called by trumpet to assemble in the King's streets and the open square. Let the prince lead the King's horse through the streets, with the man whom the King would honor mounted on a jeweled saddle, holding reins of gold in his hand. Let the prince proclaim to all the people: 'This is the man whom the King delights to honor.'"

"Good!" said the King. "You are the noble prince who can carry this out for one who saved the King's life and has not been honored. Go now, take the royal robe, the crown, and dress Mordecai, the King's jeweler, in them. Mount him upon the King's horse, and in the streets and the open square proclaim the words you have spoken. See that it is carried out as you have so well advised. Omit nothing."

Haman was surprised, frightened, bewildered, and angry. He had come to the palace for permission to hang Mordecai. Now he is ordered to carry out the details of a parade of honor for him which Haman had designed for himself.

But there was no turning back. Haman now began to fear misfortune for himself. He, therefore, carried out all that the King had ordered for Mordecai.

Except for Haman's call to the people, "This is the man whom the King delights to honor," no words were spoken between Haman and Mordecai. When Haman and his attendants had arrived to prepare Mordecai for the parade, Mordecai had thought it mockery before his execution as he had seen done to others who were doomed. Haman had decided that Mordecai would be the first Jew to die. Esther had failed.

Not until he had ridden through the streets and the parade was finished at the Gate of the Golden Spearmen, did Mordecai know that he was not to hang on the newly erected scaffold. At the Gate of the Golden Spearmen, Haman sent the King's horse, robe, and crown back to the palace by an attendant; and Haman hurried to his own house, leaving Mordecai at the gate among his friends.

"At last the King remembered to honor the one who saved his life," Mordecai's friends shouted as they crowded around to make him speak. But Mordecai, deeply puzzled, thinking the King was paying one last debt to a single Jew before they all were destroyed, went to his favorite place to pray and look longingly at the Queen's palace.

In his own house Haman was a shaken and troubled man; so much so that Zeresh and his advisers listened sympathetically to all that had happened to him.

"If I could only get the gallows removed before the King sees it," Haman lamented, "he would never know the purpose for which I came to the court at dawn."

Then the wise counselor who had brought Shekthar from the Counting House to tell Haman the story of Daniel spoke, "If the King is showing favor to Mordecai, the Jew whom you despise, removal of the gallows will not end your troubles and fears. And if Mordecai's God is the God of Daniel, you have already begun to fall."

Haman rose to drive the wise one from his presence. At the door the wise one passed the King's attendants who had come to take Haman to dine with the Queen.

Haman was hastened away to the palace. His troubled morning had caused him to forget the invitation. The people in the bazaar at the end of the Street of Awnings bowed down as he passed. Over their bent backs he glimpsed Mordecai standing erect under the awning of his shop.

In the Queen's palace Esther had heard nothing of the honor that had come to Mordecai. She had sent neither Hegai nor Hathach into the street since the days of fasting and prayer began.

As she sat at wine with the King and Haman, she

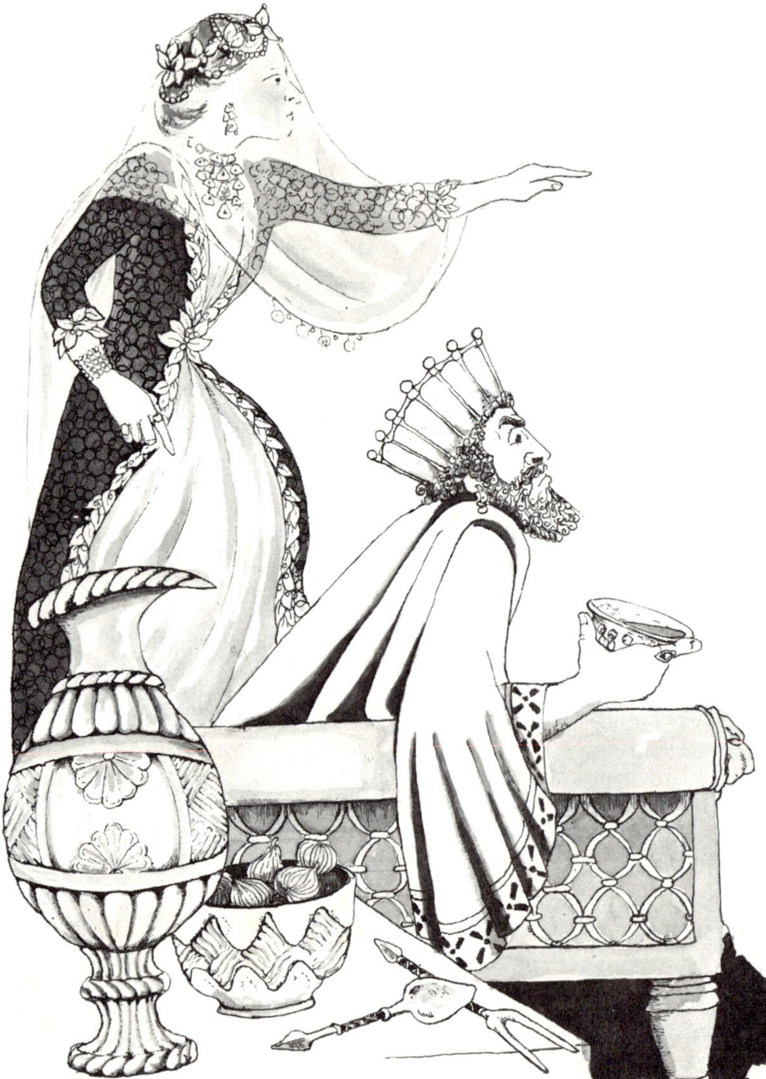

studied Haman carefully. He seemed to flatter the King less with his beginning salutation of the day before, "O King, my lord" repeated often. Indeed Haman, who had spent much time yesterday also flattering the beautiful Queen, having no idea that she was a Jewess, was very quiet.

It was during one of these periods of silence that the King spoke gently to Esther, "What is your petition, Queen Esther? It shall be granted you. And your request. Even if it be half of my Kingdom, it shall be granted."

Esther spoke with quiet courage, not once turning her eyes toward Haman: "If I have found favor in your sight, O King, and if it please the King, let my life and the lives of my people be given us, for we are marked for destruction. You chose me for your Queen from among many peoples of all the vast lands over which you rule. You did not say to me: Are you a Jew? Are you an Armenian, a Syrian, an Arab, or a Greek? You only asked that I be your helpmate and honor and obey the King. All this I have done. But now we are sold, I and my people, to be slain and annihilated, even to the last helpless infant.

"If we had been merely sold as slaves to enrich the King's treasury in time of trouble, I would have held my peace, for our affliction is not to be compared to the King's need."

Xerxes had remained motionless and speechless, unable to believe his own ears. Now he leaped from his couch, asking, "Who is he, and where is he, who would dare do such a thing?"

"Our enemy is this wicked Haman," Esther replied. And now Esther, composed and beautiful, looked straight at Haman.

The King's anger at having been tricked by Haman now rose to the height of fury. He dashed upon Haman, then turned quickly and went into the palace garden lest he strangle him in the Queen's presence.

Haman fell on his knees before the Queen's couch, and in his frenzied pleas for mercy, began tugging hard at her robes. Xerxes returning, thought Haman was attacking Esther, so he called his guards to subdue Haman and take him away.

It was at this moment that Harbona, one of the King's counselors who was a Nubian and a friend of Hegai, came forward and spoke to the King, perhaps at Hegai's prompting: "Is it known to you, O King, that Haman built a gallows on which to hang Mordecai whom the King honored?"

"Take Haman and hang him on gallows he built for Mordecai. Bring Mordecai to the palace," the King ordered.

In the presence of Esther and his friend Hegai, Mordecai was elevated to Haman's position, and when the King gave him Haman's signet ring with which he could seal royal orders, the King said to him, "Prepare first an order to provide your people, the Jews, protection, and seal it with Haman's seal."

Esther, the orphan Queen, had saved her people. For more than two thousand years they have celebrated her victory with a feast of thanksgiving, called the Feast of Purim.‡

---

‡ The name of the holiday comes from the Persian word *Pur*, meaning to cast lots. (In our day to throw dice or flip a coin.) Haman was so calloused and heartless that he laughingly cast lots to decide the month and day for carrying out his bloody orgy of extermination.

The feast begins at evening the thirteenth of the Jewish month of Adar (our late February or early March) and continues through the fourteenth. The story of Esther is read. Gifts are given to the poor. It is a festival of rejoicing and thanksgiving.

WILLIAM H. ARMSTRONG received the Newbery Medal in 1970 for his novel *Sounder* and the Mark Twain Award in 1972. His other books include *Study Is Hard Work, Peoples of the Ancient World, 87 Ways to Help Your Child in School, Through Troubled Waters, Sour Land, Animal Tales,* and *Barefoot in the Grass: The Story of Grandma Moses.* He teaches ancient history and study techniques at Kent School in Kent, Connecticut, where he lives on a sheep farm.